T0343620

HOW TO
SUPPORT
YOUR
ANXIOUS
CHILD

HOW TO SUPPORT YOUR ANXIOUS CHILD

An Hachette UK Company
www.hachette.co.uk

Vie Books, an imprint of Summersdale Publishers Ltd
Part of Octopus Publishing Group Limited
Carmelite House
50 Victoria Embankment
LONDON
EC4Y 0DZ
UK

www.summersdale.com

Printed and bound in Poland

ISBN: 978-1-83799-167-9

Substantial discounts on bulk quantities of Summersdale books are available to corporations, professional associations and other organizations. For details contact general enquiries: telephone: +44 (0) 1243 771107 or email: enquiries@summersdale.com.

Neither the author nor the publisher can be held responsible for any injury, loss or claim – be it health, financial or otherwise – arising out of the use, or misuse, of the suggestions made herein. None of the opinions or suggestions in this book are intended to replace medical opinion. If you have concerns about your health or that of a child in your care, please seek professional advice.

By bestselling author
Poppy O'Neill

HOW TO
SUPPORT
YOUR
ANXIOUS
CHILD

A Practical Guide for Parents and Carers

Contents

Introduction

We all experience anxiety – it's a normal, healthy human emotion. But when anxiety starts to become overwhelming it can impact our quality of life, physical health and relationships. If your child is becoming more withdrawn or seems to be preoccupied by their thoughts, it's time to be proactive and find ways to manage and regulate their anxiety so they can live a calmer, happier life. If you have serious concerns about your child's mental health, or you are feeling the strain yourself, seeking help from a doctor is a good idea, and professional advice can be supported by self-help, such as the tools and strategies you'll find in this book.

Anxiety can affect anyone and it can follow a troubling experience or come seemingly out of nowhere. The most common types of anxiety experienced by children and young people are separation anxiety, specific phobias, social anxiety and school anxiety. However, it's also possible for children to feel a more general sense of anxiety that seems to be present all or most of the time.

The way anxiety functions and manifests is unique to everyone, but you may recognize some of these common signs in your child...

- Reluctance to try new things

- Inability to cope with everyday challenges

- Finding it hard to concentrate

- Trouble sleeping or eating properly

- Prone to angry outbursts

- Frequent irritability

- Distressing thoughts

- Excessive worry about future events

- Seeking constant reassurance

- Feeling tense most of the time

If these traits sound familiar, don't panic. As a parent or carer you are in an excellent position to support and guide your child through difficulties, giving them the right tools and a better emotional awareness that will help them grow into resilient, compassionate young adults. Take a look at the tips in this book and use them as a guide to support your child.

How to Use This Book

If you've picked up this book, it's likely you're one of a growing number of parents and carers concerned about their child's emotional health. Recent studies have found that one in eight children and young people aged 5–19 have a mental health disorder, with 7.2 per cent of children suffering from an anxiety disorder. While your child may or may not suffer with anxiety to this degree, it's important to give children the tools to regulate their emotions in order to grow into healthy, confident young people.

Anxiety can present quite differently depending on age group – for example, younger children may have stomach aches or tantrums, while older children and teens more commonly express anxiety via anger, defiance or emotional withdrawal.

Taking a holistic approach and drawing on a variety of methods – including proven talking therapies such as CBT and ways to develop coping strategies, along with advice on relaxation, mindfulness and nutrition – this book aims to help parents understand their child's anxiety and offers inspiration on how to manage and reduce it.

Every child is different, so pick and choose the tips that appeal to you and work best for your child.

Chapter 1

TALKING

AND

LISTENING

One of the hardest parts about parenting an anxious child is that they often don't yet have the language to articulate how they feel, especially when they are panicking. Worries about how others might react can also make your child reluctant to express themselves.

In this chapter we'll look at how to start a conversation with your child about how they are feeling.

Finding the right time and place to talk

Sitting down with your child to "have a chat" might not be the best strategy, as it could feel unnatural and intimidating to them. Try to broach the subject while you're doing a calm activity, just the two of you. Perhaps gardening, walking, cooking or colouring together. Having something else to focus on, and less eye contact, can make tricky conversations flow more easily.

Take the pressure right off and don't push if they don't want to talk or can't articulate what's wrong. Have patience, trust your gut and let them take the lead.

How to listen

The right kind of listening will mean your child feels safe expressing themselves to you. Let them have their say and respond by using body language to show you are listening and understanding. When the moment's right, paraphrase what they have said, showing they have your full attention. It's important to remember that you don't need to agree with your child – a lot of worries can be irrational – but you can still affirm and empathize with them.

Try these phrases:

"I hear you."

"I can see why that would make you feel sad/worried/upset."

"That makes sense."

"How does that feel in your body?"

This technique is called active listening and it's used by therapists to encourage the speaker to open up.

What is normal for your child?

Your gut instinct is second to none when it comes to your child. If something feels wrong or different, trust that feeling, even if you can't quite put your finger on it.

Try to pinpoint what has changed. Consider your child's daily routine, their mood, language, behaviour and reaction to everyday events. Make a brief note of before and after you noticed a change. It's also worth chatting to other adults in your child's life – their teacher for example – to get a fuller picture.

It might be the case that your child is struggling to cope with a life event – like moving house, being ill, starting a new school, being bullied or losing a loved one. Our reactions to these things can be delayed or seem unrelated, so keep an open mind and consider all possibilities.

Reading between the lines

If your child insists nothing is wrong, it's worth considering what barriers there may be to expressing themselves fully. Often children might be worried about angering or upsetting you, so you can try reassuring them in advance. If you've reacted emotionally to something they've told you before, first of all forgive yourself. Acknowledge it to your child and apologize: "I know I got angry that time we talked before, and that was wrong of me. I'm sorry and I promise I won't get angry with you this time."

The aim is to let your child feel safe and unpressured, so don't ever push them to talk. Trust that they will come to you when they're ready.

When your child can't put it into words

Talking isn't the only way we humans have of communicating and feelings can often be expressed more comfortably in other, more creative ways. Try these alternative communication tools:

- Writing poetry or a letter

- Drawing

- Playing out scenarios in an age-appropriate way using toys, fictional characters or role play

- Using emojis – have a selection to choose from pinned up in your kitchen or use text messages if your child has a phone

If you feel uncomfortable with what your child expresses, it's useful to remember that research has found expressing difficult emotions through creative play is one of the most effective ways for children to process their feelings and improve their mental health.

Bonding

Find activities you and your child enjoy doing together and do more of them! It might be as simple as doing a food shop, watching a favourite TV show or playing a board game – do not underestimate the power of these shared moments. They are the foundation of communication and trust.

Make time each week for bonding and let the conversation flow naturally. Talk about everything and anything and your child will feel able to share their mental and emotional struggles with you too.

How to talk about emotions

Emotions are a part of being human. Life would be incredibly boring without them! The aim is not to avoid feeling negative emotions, rather to ride them out, accept them and let them go.

All emotions – both positive and negative – are temporary. And all emotions are valid. How your child is feeling can never be "wrong". Sometimes emotions can lead to behaviours that aren't safe, so it's really important to separate these out (see page 119).

Let your child know that it's OK to feel however they are feeling. It's OK to cry, to laugh, to frown, and that it is not your child's job to be happy all the time.

How to talk about anxiety

Whatever the age of your child, you can explain why we feel anxiety in terms of evolution and biology. Here's a simple way of putting it:

"Anxiety is a type of fear or worry. It's really useful for keeping us safe by stopping us from doing dangerous things. But sometimes our brains aren't able to tell the difference between real and imaginary danger, so they produce feelings of anxiety in our bodies just in case."

The emotion of anxiety often brings with it uncomfortable sensations and thoughts. Ask your child: "How does it feel in your body? Can you point to where you feel it? What thoughts are in your mind?"

Feel free to research anxiety in more depth with your child – the Mind and Anxiety UK websites are a good place to start. The better their understanding, the more equipped they'll be to cope with it.

Identifying triggers

You can probably list the things that trigger your child's anxiety. Times of day, situations or even a particular person might cause their stress levels to rise.

Try to identify these triggers and talk to your child about them. Ask: "When this happens, how do you feel?"

If there are many triggers, try to look for a unifying theme; this could be social situations, changing clothes, speaking to adults... the underlying anxiety will be particular to your child.

Rather than avoiding these situations altogether, see if you can take some of the pressure off and make your child more comfortable. Ask your child for their ideas and make suggestions. Try to work together to come up with solutions, letting your child take an active role in managing their anxiety.

When your child is panicking

When humans feel high anxiety, our rational brains can shut down. In addition to shortness of breath, a need to hide and a racing heartbeat, often the outward signs of a panic attack in children might be labelled as bad behaviour. It helps to shift your perception and view it as an involuntary expression of panic rather than "acting out".

An anxiety attack is an ever-changing situation, so you need to stay calm, move with it and be intuitive. One moment your child might need to be spoken to in a clear, firm voice; the next, they're ready for a hug.

Do not expect your child to make sense or be articulate. Resist the impulse to lecture, question or shame your child. You can discuss any problematic behaviour later, right now your focus is to help your child regulate their emotions and feel safe again.

Don't take it personally

What your child tells you might be hard for you to hear. Remember, they are dealing with big emotions and may find it hard to express themselves. Children are also naturally very self-centred and lack impulse control. It's important you don't take their words to heart, blame yourself or start to believe you are a bad parent.

Try to let go of any harsh words your child might say to you and focus on the underlying feeling. Your child needs to know that you love them no matter what. (If they say something that's unacceptable to you, speak to them about it later, when you are both feeling calm.)

Keep the focus on your child and know that they are talking about their own inner world, even when their words are directed outward.

Shift your language

It's important to treat your child as an individual at all times. Try to shift from labelling your child to labelling the emotion or behaviour you're talking about. For example, instead of "You're a worrier", say "It seems like you're feeling anxious/worried right now."

This shift in language will help your child understand that their emotions do not define them, nor are they a permanent part of their personality.

We all experience anxiety to a greater or lesser extent. The trick is to not attach ourselves to the feeling and let it pass naturally.

What not to say

It's common to try to help minimize your child's difficult emotions with reassuring language. We're used to squashing down or ignoring difficult feelings in the hope that they'll go away – but this doesn't work!

Phrases to avoid:

- It's no big deal
- Just go to sleep
- I'll do it for you

All of these phrases try to solve the problem without actually addressing your child's anxiety. Hearing these messages, your child will believe that their feelings are not valid, making them less likely to express themselves.

What to say instead

Instead of attempting to sweep away your child's worries with logic or reassurance, acknowledge and show understanding for their emotions. Even if they're not able to articulate how they're feeling, you can make an educated guess to help them feel understood.

Say something like: "You're feeling really worried. This feels really difficult and you're not sure what's going to happen."

Alternatively, you could speak about how you might feel in a similar situation: "If that happened to me I'd feel quite scared that it would happen again."

When we show our children that we see their emotions and that we're not upset or afraid of them, they are reassured that we're on their team and can handle challenges together.

Advocating for your child

Often, and especially when it comes to anxiety around social situations or school, it's necessary for us to advocate for or speak on behalf of our children. Some children find it very difficult to speak up when they're feeling anxious, so knowing when and how to respectfully speak up for them is a valuable skill.

This might be speaking to a teacher about the things your child struggles with, suggesting strategies that help or informing them of the signs that denote your child is becoming overwhelmed. Or it could take the form of speaking up for your child when you can tell they're in an uncomfortable situation – both to help others understand and to help your child relax or leave the situation.

When your child knows you've got their back, they'll feel less alone and more able to face potentially difficult situations.

Chapter 2

CALMING

ACTIVITIES

TO TRY WITH

YOUR CHILD

Relaxing is a life skill and it comes more naturally to some than others. Children who struggle with anxiety might need a little extra help learning what works for them and how to relax properly, so take a look at the ideas in this chapter and try out a few to see what works.

Make a calming playlist

The tunes that relax us vary from person to person. For you it might be classical music that soothes a frazzled mind but for your child only dance music will do. Human tastes rarely make sense so go with whatever works for your child and try not to judge. You might like to try an app for affirmations (short, positive, repetitive messages), guided meditations (recorded instructions to focus on while meditating) or audiobooks if music isn't quite right.

Help them compile a relaxation playlist to plug in to whenever they need a break from their thoughts.

Mind- and body-calming activities

Research has found that repeated, rhythmic activities work to relax and rewire the link between a child's brain and their nervous system, making it easier for them to regulate their emotions.

Rhythmic activities include:

- Walking
- Dancing
- Running
- Bouncing on a trampoline
- Drumming
- Singing
- Yoga
- Breathing exercises

When your child is in the company of an adult they trust and feel comfortable with, a little of one or more of these activities every day can have a marked effect on their mental health, according to research carried out by American psychiatrist Dr Bruce Perry.

Reading

Getting lost in a book is a wonderful way to relax and escape the real world for a while. Research has found that after just six minutes of reading, stress levels are reduced by up to 68 per cent.* What's more, recent studies have discovered that reading fiction can improve your capacity for self-compassion. When we feel compassion for ourselves, we're kinder and more accepting of our quirks and emotions, which leads to decreased anxiety.

Research popular books in the right age group and take your child to a library or bookshop to choose a few. There's something out there for every child and many novels for young people come as part of a series, so there'll be no shortage of reading material once they've found their niche.

*Source: University of Sussex

Colouring

Try a colouring book. Colouring has been found to have the same health benefits as meditation, allowing your child's brain to switch off and focus on one thing, which in turn reduces anxiety and restores a sense of well-being. Regularly indulging in a simple, creative activity like colouring is a powerful tool for creating a calmer mind.

There are lots and lots of colouring books out there for all ages and tastes, so take the time to choose one that will appeal to your child. Pair it with a fresh pack of felt tips or colouring pencils for a truly special gift.

One-minute meditation

—

Try reading this simple meditation to your child, while they sit or lie somewhere warm and comfortable:

Breathe normally and relax your face. Close your eyes. Relax your shoulders, your arms, your tummy, your hips, your legs and your toes. Imagine yourself as a circular pool of water.

Thoughts or feelings might make ripples appear on your surface, but each one calms and disappears without effort. Beneath the surface you are always still, clear water. Perhaps there are small bright fish in the pool, can you follow them? They swim in slow circles, weaving through swaying green plants. Gentle beams of sunlight sparkle through the water. When you're ready, follow one of the fish up to the surface – you can wiggle your toes to help you. Now, wiggle your bottom and shoulders, turn your head from side to side and slowly open your eyes.

Being in nature

Studies show fresh air has a calming effect on the body and mind, reducing the heart rate and stress considerably. There is always a lot to see and do in any green space, so why not visit your nearest park or nature reserve with your child? Walking and climbing trees are excellent forms of exercise, and you can bring a little mindful attention to your surroundings by noticing the little things you come across. When you look closely, moss, seasonal finds such as conkers and acorns, small creatures, lichen and fungi are beautiful and fascinating. You could even encourage your child to take photos or sketch what they find.

Sport and exercise

Whatever your child's temperament, there's a form of exercise out there to suit them. Regular exercise has been found to reduce anxiety and build self-confidence, as well as being good for maintaining physical health and well-being. If competitive sport is their thing, look for local clubs – they often offer a free taster session.

For those who prefer a non-competitive environment there's still plenty to choose from.

Water sports and martial arts are great options to improve fitness as well as make new friends. If your child would prefer to exercise alone or with you, there are loads of yoga tutorials online for all ages, or simply pull on your running shoes and go jogging together.

Meditative hobbies

Activities where your child can use their hands in a methodical, rhythmic way have a calming effect on the brain and provide benefits such as lowered heart rate, healthier sleep patterns and improved mood – similar to meditation. Try a few simple origami designs, or invest in materials for crafts such as cross-stitch, crochet or friendship bracelet making. Toys that allow for following instructions as well as creating freely – like Lego or Hama Beads – are fun at any age. Why not join in yourself?

Spend time with animals

Being around animals has been found to reduce anxiety in children and adults. Dogs and horses are often used in therapeutic settings as they provide a non-judgemental presence that aids communication and promotes a calm atmosphere, helping children regulate their emotions.

Interacting with pets or other animals provides a non-pressurized environment in which children can express themselves. Sharing affection and speaking to animals can be a lot less daunting than doing those things with other humans!

If you have a pet, you might like to encourage your child to spend more time with it. If not, look out for local farms where kids can have hands-on experiences with the animals, or set up a regular visit with a friend's pet.

Journalling

Anxious thoughts have a habit of swirling around, repeating and amplifying themselves. Try giving your child a journal in which they can write down or draw what's on their mind. Reassure them that they don't have to write positive things, solve problems, make sense or show their journal to anyone (even you).

Try these prompts if they need a little inspiration:

- Describe or draw your emotions right now

- What thoughts are in your mind?

- What were three good things about today?

- What was the worst part of today?

The act of writing our thoughts down on paper means we can more easily let them go of them.

Grounding

Walking barefoot on grass, soil or sand has a naturally calming effect on the human body. Encourage your child to spend some time outside without shoes or socks on, and to pay attention to the sensations on the soles of their feet.

This is an exercise in mindfulness and it also puts your child in touch with the earth's natural energy, bringing their attention out of their mind and into their body. Try the exercise together and see if you can feel the difference too.

Breathing

In times of anxiety, breathing can become shallow and erratic. It might feel strange to remind your child to breathe, so try coming down to their eyeline and breathing deeply together.

Here's a simple breathing technique to teach your child:

Breathe in through your nose for five, hold for five, then breathe out through your mouth, making a sighing noise. Use your abdominal muscles to gently and completely empty your lungs.

Deep breathing helps release tension in the body, regulates levels of serotonin in the brain, improves mood and promotes a sense of well-being. If you teach your child how to breathe deeply, you'll give them a valuable relaxation tool they can use whenever and wherever they need it.

Jump around

This one might seem out of place in a chapter about relaxation, but sometimes anxious energy needs to be burned off rather than soothed.

It can be hard to persuade some children to get moving! Suggest an activity your child won't feel too silly doing. Here are a few ideas to get you started:

- Doing some jumping jacks

- Sprinting up and down the garden

- Trying out a high-energy dance routine

- Playing a ball game

- Running vigorously on the spot

Think of it as chasing away anxiety. Moving in this way gets the attention out of their head and into their body, burns off nervous energy and helps regulate their breathing.

Make a den

Some children may benefit from a "den" they can retreat to when they are feeling anxious. This could be a space under a table or even an indoor tepee. Make it cosy with cushions and blankets. It's important to discuss with your child how they want to use this space. When they are in their den, do they want to be left alone or do they want your attention? Perhaps you could make signs to hang outside, saying things like "Do not disturb", "I need a hug" or "Come and sit with me."

Being silly

When anxiety is high, it can feel like things are very serious, with no room for joy. Help your child shift out of an anxious feeling with some good old-fashioned silliness, to bring a sense of lightness and laughter into each day.

Every family has its own brand of silliness, so whether it's bringing up a hilarious shared memory, giving your pet a funny voice or lightening the mood by breaking wind, don't be afraid to inject some levity at a well-chosen moment.

It's important to note that use of silliness should not include any form of mocking of your child, or their emotions. In fact, one Italian study into humour and mental health found that fun and benevolent humour had a positive effect on worry and well-being, while use of negative humour like sarcasm and cynicism had the opposite effect.

Solving puzzles together

Brainteasers and puzzles can be a wonderful way to bond and relax with your child. Try online word or number games, or buy a book of age-appropriate puzzles you can pick up and work on together when the mood takes you.

Strike a balance between helping your child and allowing them to work things out for themselves. It's OK to pretend you need help from your child with a puzzle in order to boost their confidence; let them participate, experience trial and error and learn by doing.

Facing and solving a problem together – even if that problem is a crossword or Sudoku grid – helps foster trust, collaboration and respect between you and your child. When a higher-stakes problem crops up in your child's life, the experience of navigating these simple challenges together will help them feel confident in your ability to solve problems as a team.

Cuddle up

Studies have found that touch from our loved ones is essential to our mental health and helps reduce feelings of anxiety. Cuddles with your child are the obvious way to use touch to show we care and help them feel calm, but if your child isn't into hugs there are plenty of other ways to show them love:

- A high five or fist bump
- A gentle squeeze on the arm
- Ruffling their hair

While it may not feel like a big deal to give a hand-squeeze or tap on the shoulder, gentle touch makes a big difference to how safe and calm we feel with each other.

Shake it off

In the animal kingdom, you'll see most mammals deal with stressful or frightening situations by having a good shake straight afterwards. This works for humans too, and can be a quick way to help your child release tension and anxiety so they can relax.

Sit or stand near your child and invite them to "shake off" the anxiety with you. You could hold hands or suggest they mirror your movements – whatever feels most comfortable for the two of you. Start by wriggling your shoulders and let the rest of your body follow. Shake and wiggle each arm and leg, all the way to your fingers and toes.

Notice how your bodies feel looser, lighter and less tense after a good shake.

Stretching

Stretching releases tension held in our muscles. When we feel anxious, we can unconsciously tense our muscles – commonly in the jaw or shoulders – so stretching can help reduce your child's anxiety and find a more relaxed posture.

One of the best stretches for calming anxiety is a yoga pose called Child's Pose. It's incredibly relaxing because it releases tension in the muscles we most often tense when feeling stressed or anxious. Here's how to do it:

Kneel on the floor with your bottom resting on the soles of your feet. Spread your knees wide and walk your hands forward, lowering your head as you go. Rest your head on the floor and stretch your arms forward, or bring them to your sides – whichever feels most peaceful.

Relax and breathe deeply – you and your child can stay in Child's Pose for as long as you like.

Physical needs

While your child's anxiety exists separately from their basic bodily needs like food, water and sunlight, being without enough of these things certainly doesn't help.

A glass of water, healthy snack, toilet break or 5 minutes of fresh air helps us feel a little more relaxed, whatever the situation, so it's useful to get your child into the habit of tuning in to what their body needs.

As children get older they might not respond well to being prompted to hydrate or get some fresh air, so it's important to pitch this strategy right. Here are some ideas:

- Offer a drink or snack

- Invite them for a walk around the block

- Ask what small thing would help them feel five per cent better

Deep pressure

Many children (and adults too) respond well to what therapists call Deep Pressure Stimulation. Studies show that the feeling of firm but safe pressure on our skin has a calming effect on the nervous system. It's the theory behind why weighted blankets help soothe anxiety and there are lots of ways to try it with your child:

- Squish your child's arms and torso between two soft cushions

- Wrap them up tightly in a blanket, like a burrito

- Invest in a weighted blanket

- Bear hugs

- Cuddling a pet or weighted cuddly toy on their lap

Rather than present it as a tool for calming anxiety, it often works better if you make a game of it. Take turns being the burrito filling, see who can give the biggest hug or pretend you are making a weighted blanket lasagne.

Screens

There's little doubt that smartphones and other screens can be anxiety-provoking. But used in the right way, there's no reason relaxation time always needs to be a screen-free zone.

Here are some ideas for using screens and tech for soothing anxiety and relaxing:

- Watch a movie together
- Listen to a soothing podcast or audiobook
- Do an online puzzle with your child (see page 43)
- Try a white noise app
- Play a multiplayer game together, like virtual bowling, a co-operative video game or try a *Minecraft* building project

If your child tends to get lost in screens, this can be a coping mechanism for dealing with anxiety. While over-reliance on screens has a negative effect on children's mental health, if you have firm boundaries around screentime and the content they have access to, it's possible to create healthy habits.

Screentime

To ensure the tech and screens your child has access to support their mental well-being (or at least don't harm it), it's important to have good boundaries. Think about the length of time your child can spend on screens, what time they put them away for the night and what kind of content they have access to.

You'll probably experience pushback on these boundaries, especially if you have an older child or teenager. Here are some tips for navigating this:

- Explain that boundaries and parental controls are what enable you to give your child access to screens

- Stay firm – sometimes you need to stick to your guns, even when it upsets your child

- Be respectful – treat requests for changes to screentime rules with consideration, and if appropriate, see if you can meet in the middle

- Be empathetic – even when you're saying "no", you can still show your child understanding and empathy

Fidget toys

Anxiety can cause children to feel restless and struggle to stay still. A fidget toy – like a spinner, putty ball or silicone popping grid – can provide an outlet for these pent-up feelings, helping to lower anxiety and help kids concentrate.

There are lots of different types of fidget toy available online and in toyshops, and you can make DIY fidget toys too. Here are some simple, low-cost ideas:

- Thread fuse beads onto a jumbo paperclip
- Make an infinity cube using dice and tape
- Add beads to shoelaces or pipe cleaners and tie up the ends
- Braid stretchy fabric to make a chair-leg fidget band

If you want more details on how to make these, look at online tutorials for help.

Chapter 3

MOOD

BOOSTERS

Anxiety can bring with it a downward spiral of negativity, so it's really useful to have a few tried-and-tested tricks up your sleeve for when your child needs a boost of positivity. Try out some of these tips when you need to stop anxiety in its tracks.

Treats

Whether it's a triple choc-chip cookie or a trip to the swimming pool, you know the things that your child enjoys most in the world.

Why not create a regular family treat time, taking turns to choose so that everybody gets a chance to do their favourite thing. It doesn't have to be big or extravagant – choosing what's for dinner or which movie to watch together is a lovely treat.

While too many treats can have a negative effect, a bit of well-timed special treatment will help your child feel loved, valued and appreciated even when they're feeling low.

Play

_____

Play is essential to the healthy development of the human brain. Studies have found that play helps us learn how to navigate the unexpected, meaning the more we play the less anxiety we feel about the world around us.

Play can look different depending on the age of your child, so let them take the lead here. Make sure there is time for play every day, away from screens. Play might mean going outside with their friends, drawing, role play, building, making music – whatever your child can get absorbed in that captures their imagination is going to be an excellent antidote to stress and anxiety.

Car-e-oke

Singing has been found to reduce anxiety and release tension in the body. Belting it out to a solid-gold classic in the car is also an excellent bonding experience. You can connect without the need for conversation, be silly together and give your energy levels a boost with your choice of song. Miming and air guitar also work, just as long as you give it your all. You could even make a feel-good playlist especially for singing along to.

Duvet day

Especially when the weather outside is gloomy, try declaring the day a write-off and stay in your PJs. Snuggle up together with a feel-good movie, hot chocolate with all the trimmings and your cosiest slippers.

A day without the need to be productive will give your child a break from any pressure they might be feeling. It can be hard to take a break sometimes, especially when you're feeling anxious – the impulse is to keep moving and stay alert. A cosy, lazy day will leave your child feeling loved, rested and ready to take on the week's challenges.

Baking

Baking together is fun, creative and you get to eat the results! Try to approach baking with your child as a mindful experience. Feel the textures, concentrate on the effect of each new ingredient you add to the mix and work methodically through each stage of the recipe without rushing.

Don't worry about getting messy – clearing up together is an excellent bonding experience too.

Try low-stress recipes like flapjacks, cake pops, cookies or cupcakes for maximum yumminess and versatility, and don't forget to lick the bowl!

Helping hands

Acting altruistically releases feel-good endorphins in the brain as well as reducing stress and anxiety. There's nothing like that warm and fuzzy feeling of helping someone out with no expectation of reciprocation.

Encourage your child to bring a little altruism to their life by doing a favour for an elderly neighbour, giving away unwanted belongings, or participating in a charity cake sale or community project.

They'll learn the pleasure of giving and how it can boost even the lowest of moods.

Create a mental health shelf

Keep feel-good movies, motivational quote books, treasured photos, stress toys and soft blankets all together somewhere your child can access them whenever they need a boost.

If a shelf isn't practical, you could use a box, drawer or suitcase. You could encourage your child to personalize theirs, making it an appealing go-to place for wobbly moments. Make sure it's well stocked with familiar, comforting objects that will help restore your child's sense of well-being.

Get creative

Studies have shown that creativity is a core part of healing emotional struggles. Whatever your child's preferred medium, don't underestimate the power of exercising creativity. Try to play down the idea of good and bad, focus on the process and let them create without pressure or comparison with others.

If your child gets stuck for something to create, give them inspiration. Here are a few ideas to get their creative juices flowing:

- Your dream house

- A poster for the film of your life story

- A restaurant menu

- A magazine article about your favourite hobby

Make sure basic materials like pens, pencils and paper are always handy at home, so your child can turn to creativity whenever the mood takes them.

Expressing emotions in a healthy way

You don't have to save this one for tricky moments! We're all experiencing emotions all day long. Take a moment to ask your child (or remind them to ask themselves) this sequence of questions:

- How are you feeling?

- Can you locate the feeling in your body?

- What thoughts come along with that feeling?

- What if you let your face and body move with that feeling?

Let your child know that it's OK to cry, to express anger, to curl up, to need a hug, to refuse a hug, to speak or be silent. It's also OK to smile, laugh or dance! Stay calm and remember not to judge or take your child's emotions personally.

Laughter

Laughter relaxes our facial muscles and releases endorphins into the bloodstream, making it a fail-safe mood booster.

What makes your child laugh? It might be a particular movie, a funny face or they might love being tickled. A pillow fight or rolling down a hill are guaranteed ways to make anyone laugh.

Laughter reduces levels of cortisol in the body almost immediately and studies have shown that regular laughter increases overall feelings of well-being, even after you've finished laughing.

Tidying up

This might sound a bit optimistic, but the mental health benefits of both a tidy environment and of the act of tidying up are well-founded. Pick a small space, drawer or shelf to organize or declutter. Work together or let your child do it themselves – whichever feels right. Working your way from chaos to order is immensely satisfying and you'll both feel better for it. You could put on some upbeat music to make tidying up more of a game than a chore.

You might even rediscover some treasures along the way!

Grow something

Nurturing a plant of their own teaches your child responsibility and patience, as well as bringing a sense of satisfaction as they watch it grow and bloom or bear fruit. Give your child a plant pot, soil and seeds so they can grow their own.

Start them off with an easy-to-grow plant such as tomato, sunflower or avocado. Alternatively, you could buy a low-maintenance cactus or succulent for them to care for.

Even on this small scale, engaging with nature has been found to have a positive effect on mental health, with studies showing 90 per cent of us feel better simply by being around plants.

Get rid of negative thoughts

Bringing negative thoughts out of the mind and on to a physical object is very therapeutic, especially when you get to throw them away. Using something that's meant to be thrown away removes the seriousness attached to these thoughts.

Here are a few ideas to try:

- Use chalk to write on a stone, then throw it into the sea

- Write worries on a piece of clean toilet paper and flush it away

- Write on a piece of scrap paper and tear it into tiny pieces

Disposing of troubling thoughts in a more literal way like this can help break negative thought cycles and give your child relief from a mind that's too busy.

Get some sunshine

When the sun's out, encourage your child to spend extra time outside. Our bodies create most of our vitamin D from sunlight, which helps our brains produce the mood-enhancing chemicals serotonin and dopamine.

A walk, trip to the playground or simply sitting and feeling the sun on their face can help lift your child out of a low mood. As little as 10–15 minutes is enough to feel the benefits, but don't forget to apply sunscreen after this time has passed and stay out of the sun in the middle of the day to avoid sunburn.

Ask the expert

The opportunity to feel knowledgeable and competent will give your child a big self-esteem boost. Whatever their specialist subject is – a favourite video game universe, book series or sport – show curiosity and let them teach you all about it.

Asking an open-ended question about a topic you know they love to talk about can be a great strategy for helping some children through a potentially anxiety-inducing situation. When you sense your child starting to feel anxious, ask a question – almost any question: Are there swimming pools in *Minecraft*? Who is the most evil character in *A Series of Unfortunate Events*? If you were the manager of a football team, what would the strip look like?

Questions like this distract your child's mind from worried thoughts, helping them get through tricky moments.

Something to look forward to

———

Planning something together for the near future will give you and your child a positive future focus. It doesn't need to be an expensive trip – consider a visit to a nearby town, a DIY project or even teaming up to organize a birthday treat for another member of the family.

Involve your child in the planning process as much as possible, but don't be afraid to explain practicalities to them. If something's not good value, say so! Let them see your thought processes and allow them to participate in how adults make choices.

When children feel involved in making plans, and know their opinions will be listened to, it gives them a sense of control and possibility.

Learn a new skill

Learning a new skill is an amazing mood booster. Many children who struggle with anxiety also have perfectionist tendencies, so it can be a big challenge to stick with a new skill through those initial stumbles.

To help with this, try learning something new together. Whether it's remembering a new TikTok dance, mastering a Rubik's cube or completing a daily number puzzle, do it together so your child can see you try, make mistakes and learn from them.

Once you and your child get the hang of something new, it'll be a wonderful source of self-esteem, a chance to spend time together, not to mention an instant boost of the feel-good brain chemical, dopamine.

Be spontaneous

Anxiety often comes from the discomfort of not knowing exactly what will happen next. Our brains want our lives to be safe and predictable; but no matter how hard we try to shield our children from the unexpected, difficult challenges and surprises are a part of life.

One way we can build our children's resilience is with small, low-stake acts of spontaneity. An unplanned trip to get ice cream or an out-of-season paddle in the sea will show your child that unpredictability can feel exciting and fun, while also keeping things calm and manageable for everybody.

Many children struggle with even positive changes to their routine, so use your imagination to find out what will feel manageable and fun for your child.

Good mood food

Eating healthily can have a surprisingly positive effect on our mood. Not only does eating regular, healthy meals help us feel calm by keeping our energy levels stable, some foods have been found to actually lower anxiety, including:

- Probiotic yoghurts
- Eggs
- Citrus fruits like oranges and lemons
- Oats
- Turkey
- Sesame seeds

Adding more of these kinds of foods to your child's meals – and reducing sugar and processed food where possible – will help support them from the inside out. However, it's not worth adding to you or your child's stress if changing the food they eat is likely to bring extra anxiety.

Chapter 4

CULTIVATING

A POSITIVE

MINDSET

The way we think influences our whole life and your child is no different. Every time we challenge our usual patterns of thought, new neural pathways are created. Thinking in a new way takes practice and each time we choose a positive mindset over a negative one these new pathways are strengthened, leading to better moods, more confidence and relief from anxiety. Read on for ideas on helping your child to build positive new thought patterns.

Gratitude

Gratitude is thought to be the key to a positive outlook on life. If practised daily, gratitude can transform a negative outlook, soothe the nervous system and calm an anxious mind.

When we feel and express gratitude for big and small things, it reminds us how lucky we are, even when life isn't perfect or things feel hard.

Try listing three things you're grateful for, then see if your child can do the same. You can put anything on your gratitude list – big or small, serious or silly. Perhaps make this gratitude list a part of your breakfast routine, coming up with new things to be grateful for each day.

Role-play scenarios

If there's a particular scenario that fills your child with anxiety, it can be helpful to role-play the situation to help them shift their perspective.

Younger children might benefit more from playing out the possible outcomes using toys, while older children would probably prefer to act them out with you.

Let your child guide you – this can be an excellent way to learn about how their mind works – explore the good and bad possibilities and gently introduce more positive outcomes into the role play.

What you can and can't control

Anxious children often spend a lot of time worrying about external issues, so it might be helpful for your child to understand what they can and can't control. You could even print out a list and stick it on the wall. Try adding your own ideas to the list, specific to the things your child worries about:

What I can control:

- My words

- My actions

- My ideas

- My effort

What I can't control:

- Other people's words

- Other people's actions

- Other people's feelings

- Other people's reactions

- Other people's ideas

- Other people's effort

A simple reminder like this can help soothe your child's worried mind.

Try meditating together

Overthinking is often a feature of anxiety. It can be exhausting and very difficult to break out of a negative thought spiral. This is where meditation can come in handy. You could meditate together at the same time every week, then with practice your child can use it any time they are feeling anxious.

Ask your child to concentrate on their breathing for three deep breaths in and out, then three more. If they're struggling, it might help them to write down their thoughts first, so the thoughts can be physically put to one side.

Breathe with your child and speak calmly as you do so: "In through your nose, out through your mouth."

Keep going for a set amount of time – start with just one minute. Tell your child not to worry if their attention wanders: that is part of meditation. Gently bring it back to the breath. There is no way to be good or bad at meditation, it is simply practice.

Speak to yourself kindly

Ask your child to tune into their inner voice. We all have one and your child's might be particularly unkind, critical or fearful. You can often hear your child's inner voice when they feel they have messed up or are about to do something daunting. Look out for absolutes like "always" and "never" – these can be signs of a bullying inner voice.

Ask your child: would you talk to your best friend in that way? If the answer is no, then they should adjust their self-talk to include compassion and understanding toward themselves.

It's easier said than done, but with practice your child can learn to ignore the inner bullies and choose to believe their inner best friend instead.

Thoughts aren't facts

Just because your child thinks they are going to fail, does not make it true. Achieving a more positive mindset is a slow process and must be done one thought at a time.

You can think of thoughts like stories. They might hold some truth, but there's always another way of telling the story.

For example, you might change the story "I am going to fail" into "I am going to try my best", "I am going to succeed" or "If I'm not perfect, I will be OK."

Try a few different thought stories and see which feels comfortable for your child.

Positive thinking

Cultivating a positive or "growth" mindset will help free your child from the idea that past mistakes are likely to recur.

A growth mindset values experience and imperfection over getting things right first time. Instead of "I can't do this", it says "I can't do this yet."

Getting something 100 per cent right first time feels amazing, but it's often down to luck. When we make mistakes or fail, that is when we truly learn. Encourage your child to see failure as an essential part of success and each mistake or setback as an opportunity to improve and grow.

Self-belief

Anxiety can stem from a child's lack of trust in their own judgement and abilities. Look at it this way: if you believe you can handle setbacks, you don't worry so much about what might go wrong.

Try giving your child some simple, age-appropriate responsibilities, something they feel comfortable being in charge of. They might roll their eyes, but this is about more than chores! It will show your child that you trust them. When they see that they are able to perform these tasks – and that what they do matters and is appreciated by others – it will boost their levels of self-belief.

Each child is different, and you know their capabilities and strengths best. Here are some ideas for responsibilities you could give a child:

Ages 5–9:

- Growing a plant from a seed
- Putting away their own clean laundry
- Picking a family film

Ages 10–12:

- Caring for a section of the garden
- Clearing the table after dinner
- Washing the car

Age 12+

- Saving up for a big purchase
- Walking the family dog
- Cooking dinner once a week

Challenging anxious thoughts

There are patterns to anxious thinking that are often referred to as "thinking errors". Here are some of the most common, with ideas for how you can gently challenge your child if and when they express similar thoughts.

Catastrophizing:

"The worst is going to happen and everything will be ruined." "OK, that's one possibility. Let's come up with some others."

Black-and-white thinking:

"If one person doesn't want to be my friend, no one will." "It hurts when that happens. Let's try thinking about this another way – do you like every person you meet?"

Fortune-telling:

"I just know that today is going to be a disaster." "And if it is, you'll be OK. What would it be like if today goes well?"

The idea here is not to tell your child that their feelings are wrong on unjustified, but to invite them to see things a different way.

Perfectionism

Perfectionism can be paralyzing. Anxiety born of perfectionism will stop your child from trying new things, being creative and reaching their full potential.

A good antidote to perfectionism is seeing a role model being imperfect. Believe it or not, you are a role model for your child. So, feel free to mess up and make mistakes sometimes. Take a wrong turn and find your way back on track, trip over and laugh about it – it's all about how you respond to your own imperfections.

You will cope

When your child expresses worry about something that might happen, it can be tempting to dismiss the worry and explain how unlikely it is. However, statistics won't calm an anxious mind. There is always the possibility that it might happen, and that's what keeps the anxious thought swirling around in your child's head.

Instead, try reassuring your child that even if something bad does happen, they will cope. You could make an action plan of ways to keep calm and solve the problem; or role-play the scenario, letting your child take the lead. This can be a gentle way to help your child face their fears.

Comparison

A lot of childhood anxiety can come from observing other children and comparing yourself with them. This is perfectly normal and it's almost certain that every other child is doing the same! It's also very likely that other children secretly admire qualities in your child. Remind them of this when they feel inferior to their peers in some way.

Let your child know that they are wonderful exactly as they are and that what other people do, look like or achieve does not diminish or build up your child's worth.

Only ever two things to do

When your child is feeling overwhelmed, remind them that there are only ever two things to do: the first is breathe and the second is the task in front of them.

It might be helpful to break down whatever they are struggling to do into smaller parts, like the question they are working on or the next few steps they take.

What's more, the task in front of them can almost always wait, so breathing becomes the only thing on their to-do list for a little while.

This exercise is a useful way of bringing your child's mind back to the present moment and away from anxious thoughts about the past or future.

Get interested in thoughts

It can be useful to teach your child a strategy to quieten their thoughts. You could remember the acronym N.A.I.L. which stands for:

Name it, **A**ccept it, get **I**nterested, **L**et it go

When a troubling or anxious thought or feeling arises, your child can:

Name it by saying (to themselves or out loud) "I'm feeling X."

Accept it by allowing it, knowing that it cannot hurt them and will pass.

Get **interested** in the feeling or thought: What has triggered it? Where in their body can they feel it? What is it telling them?

Then when the thought or feeling is ready to pass, **let it go** without trying to push it away or cling to it.

This exercise can be done in your child's head, out loud, written in a journal or on a piece of scrap paper. It's good to introduce this kind of practice when they are calm, as it can be helpful with any emotion.

Phobias

A phobia is an extreme or irrational fear, and sometimes children's anxiety comes from a place that seems irrational – for example, a monster under the bed. It's worth remembering that a child's idea of what's rational and irrational is not as developed as an adult's. These things don't feel outlandish to your child!

It's tempting to dismiss this kind of worry as "silly". But try to look past the object of your child's anxiety and focus on the emotion itself. What your child is really asking is for you to soothe them. It's important to validate how they are feeling. You could use phrases like, "That sounds really frightening." Or ask questions like, "How does it feel in your body right now?" Or even, "What colour pyjamas does the monster wear?"

However, if a phobia is starting to have a negative impact on your child's day-to-day life, it's best to make an appointment to discuss it with your doctor.

Common phobias

Phobias can come in many forms, and these are the most common types of phobia among children:

- A type of person or animal, e.g. clowns or dogs
- A place or type of place, e.g. elevators or graveyards
- Objects, e.g. needles or balloons
- Activities, e.g. swimming or riding a bike
- Situations, e.g. getting lost or being without their comfort blanket

Whatever the specific fear your child struggles with, it's important to show them that you understand and are on their team. Be creative in how you can gently encourage them to face these fears, without overwhelming them. For example, for a child who is afraid of dogs, a book featuring a heroic or lovable dog could help shift how they think about real dogs.

Don't avoid the negative

It can be really tempting to avoid mentioning any negative aspects of your child's life, instead focusing on positivity and resilience. While this is an understandable impulse and comes from a loving place, our children need to know that we understand their challenges and how significant they feel.

Perhaps there's a test coming up at school. You want to give your child pep talks and help them schedule in revision, but what they might need even more from you is an acknowledgement of the pressure they feel, or how worried they are about the test.

Bringing up something you suspect is bothering your child will not cause them more anxiety about it. In all likelihood, it's already playing on their mind. If you guess what's troubling them correctly, it will be a huge relief for them. And if you get it wrong, no big deal.

Notice patterns

Sometimes, the root of a child's anxiety is hard to pin down. Their anxious behaviours might seem unpredictable or random, leaving you struggling to work out what might help them.

In situations like this, noticing patterns can be helpful. Keep a journal or note on your phone of the times, places and situations where your child feels heightened anxiety. If they're going through or nearing puberty, it's worth considering hormone cycles too. Look for possible links between each situation – perhaps there's a risk of rejection, the potential for loss of control or they're reminded of a troubling memory.

When you zoom out a little and look for patterns, it can reveal a deeper meaning behind your child's struggles with anxiety.

A part of me...

Speaking about our anxieties can be a big challenge for both adults and children. We often experience conflicting thoughts, a fear of sounding silly or of offending others.

Anything that separates ourselves from our emotions can help with expressing them. The phrase "a part of me..." can be very helpful here. The easiest way to encourage your child to use this strategy is to do it yourself. You could say...

> **"A part of me feels quite nervous about the party, but another part of me is really looking forward to it."**

> **"A part of me wants to hide behind the sofa when the scary part of this film is coming up!"**

> **"A part of me thinks it's easier to stay at home this weekend, but I don't want to miss out on a trip to the beach."**

When your child sees you expressing conflicting emotions, it becomes easier for them to follow suit.

What if...

Children are naturally creative. Unfortunately, this means their anxieties are too. A feeling of anxiety combined with a big imagination can lead your child to picture all sorts of disasters and unlikely outcomes.

One way to redirect your child's wonderful imagination away from anxious thoughts is to ask, "What if?"

"What if something funny happens instead?"

"What if we were secret agents?"

"What if everything works out perfectly?"

While this won't necessarily break them out of an anxious thought pattern, a gentle challenge to a typically quite rigid thought process can help show your child that alternative thoughts are available to them. With a bit of practice, your child can even learn to recognize and interrupt their own negative thought patterns.

You make sense

Children who struggle with anxiety can be pretty hard on themselves. It can be frustrating when feelings and thoughts get in the way of living your life, and many children end up blaming themselves or believing they just need to "get over" their feelings of anxiety.

Take the time to give your child credit for the challenges they're up against, whether it's starting a new school, being bullied, caring responsibilities, or simply the challenge of dealing with heightened anxiety. Let them know that it makes perfect sense that they find certain things stressful, and that you understand how difficult life can be for them.

When you acknowledge these factors out loud, you give your child permission to be a bit kinder to themselves.

Realistic goals

Does your child tend to aim high, expect a lot of themselves, then end up stressed, disappointed and upset when they don't live up to their own impossible standards? This is a hard lesson to learn and a real challenge for bright, ambitious kids.

Perhaps your child felt inspired by a painting, tried to recreate it and felt discouraged when their picture didn't look quite the same as the original.

We can help our children set realistic goals and expectations when we add context to others' achievements. In the painting example, you could point out that an artist reached the height of their talent by first learning about paint colours and how to mix them.

When you show your child that achievements take time, involve experimenting and sometimes failing, and that they are capable of learning pretty much anything, they can set realistic expectations and appreciate their progress.

Baby steps

When it comes to facing fears, less is more. If we try to do too much, too soon, it can feel overwhelming and set us back in lessening our anxiety. For example, a child afraid of being alone in the dark will probably feel considerably more scared of the dark if they are made to sleep without a light on before they feel ready.

Instead, think in terms of baby steps. How could you support your child to take one small step toward their fear? If it's being alone in the dark that brings them high anxiety, a night light might be that first step. If your child is afraid of dogs, a brief, positive interaction with a very calm dog might help.

Once you've taken a first step, keep the next step just as small. Anxiety fades when we gently expand our comfort zone – there's no rush.

Chapter 5

CREATING A

CALM HOME

ENVIRONMENT

Children are especially sensitive to the world around them and a calm environment is more conducive to a calm mind. This chapter looks at some of the less obvious factors that can affect our mood. A few tweaks toward a more peaceful atmosphere at home can make a big difference.

Eating well

What your child puts in their body has an effect on their mood. Excessive sugar, salt and processed foods can lead to tiredness, irritability and increased anxiety. Kids can be fussy and it's important not to turn meals into a battleground, so try to work with the foods they're already fond of and familiar with. Go for low-sugar alternatives (but look for natural sweeteners rather than chemical additives) to their favourite treats, make sure their favourite fruit is always in the fruit bowl and go easy with the salt shaker while cooking. Small, healthy changes such as these can help your child regulate their mood throughout the day.

Staying hydrated

Dehydration has been found to increase levels of the stress hormone cortisol. Its effects – increased heart rate, a dry mouth, dizziness and headaches – can also mimic those of anxiety, meaning your child might feel heightened anxiety simply because they don't have enough water in their bodies. It's worth treating your child to a water bottle they're proud to be seen sipping from, which will encourage them to stay hydrated. A big gulp of water is an instant mood-booster and adequate hydration helps regulate emotions, as well as improve sleep and digestion.

Stretch

Stretching releases tension held in your body, giving an instant boost of calming energy. A simple stretch such as reaching up toward the ceiling is a good habit for your child to get into first thing in the morning, when many of us instinctively want to stretch.

You could also try out some yoga moves with your child, such as Cat, Cow or Child's Pose. Search online for kids' yoga moves or find a local class. Encourage your child to stretch whenever they are feeling tense or anxious – it will help to release excess tension and balance their mood.

Switching off for sleep

Anxiety can have a huge effect on sleep and a child who struggles to sleep has a huge effect on the rest of the household! Learning how to relax and set worries aside at night is a valuable life skill. Make sure your child has a good, predictable bedtime routine in place (see page 113), including self-care and screen-free time.

You might notice your child seeking attention in numerous ways around bedtime. Try to stay calm in your response to these bids for attention. Whether it's "I'm thirsty", "One more page" or "There's a monster under my bed", what your child is really asking for is your reassurance.

Respond to your child with warmth and patience but keep it brief. If it feels right, you might like to say something like, "You're feeling scared." This will help them open up, express their feelings of anxiety and relax more.

Each time you respond to your child, their trust that you are there for them when they need you grows. Perhaps counter-intuitively, the more they feel sure that you'll come when they call, the less they'll call.

It's important to note that it's not through any lack in your parenting that they feel anxiety at bedtime. In terms of evolution, being alone while sleeping wasn't a good idea thousands of years ago when we were vulnerable to threats such as wild animals. Even though we're safe from these threats now, our emotional brains have not entirely lost this instinct.

Make your home a place of positivity

Try putting positive messages around your home where your child can see them.

Postcards, Post-it notes, pages from magazines or your favourite quotes – you can find positivity anywhere. Whenever you see a calming, uplifting or soothing message, write it down, cut it out or print it, stick it on your fridge, wall, or pin it to a noticeboard.

Seeing short, memorable words of positivity on a regular basis as they go about their day will help give your child little boosts.

Routine

Children like to know what to expect and what is expected of them. Sticking to a regular routine at the beginning and end of the day will help your child feel calm, comfortable and in control.

If there's a particular time of day or part of the routine that brings your child heightened anxiety, you can break it down even more. Give this part of the day extra time to remove pressure and speak calmly about the task at hand. For example, if going into school is a stressful time for your child, remind them that cleaning their teeth, putting on their shoes or walking to the end of the road are all they need to do at that moment. Take the routine one step at a time and keep calm.

Create a healthy relationship with screens

Screen-based entertainment increases arousal in the central nervous system, which can exacerbate anxiety, so it's a good idea to place limits on both the amount of time your child spends using computers or watching TV, as well as paying attention to the ways in which they are using technology.

It's hard to find a balance, especially as more and more schoolwork and communication has become computer-based. Read up on internet safety at www.internetmatters. org and aim to create a safe, age-appropriate attitude toward screens for yourself and your child. Focus on quality rather than quantity, making sure your child uses technology in a positive and responsible way.

Look for ways you can use technology to connect with each other, such as games you can play together. Try to model healthy screen use by setting clear boundaries that everyone in the house is expected to stick to.

Self-care

Learning to take responsibility for looking after their own physical needs to a certain degree helps give children a sense of control and trust in themselves. Although it can often be quicker to do things yourself – like cleaning teeth or brushing hair for younger children and making food and drinks for older ones – try to loosen the reins a little when it comes to self-care.

Make sure everything they need is accessible to them – low down enough for them to reach or kept in their own bedroom, for example – and show them how to do it until they feel confident enough to try it alone. If they get stuck, you can give a little help if needed, but let your child learn how to recognize and tend to their own needs.

Downtime

Modern life can get hectic. With after-school activities, weekend clubs and homework eating into their free time, our kids are busier than ever too.

If you sense your child is overcommitted, see what can be cut. Ask whether each activity is worth the time, headspace and energy it requires of them.

More free time means more time for unstructured play, relaxation and creativity, more opportunities to be spontaneous, to connect with each other or to simply breathe and be in the moment.

Social anxiety

Feelings of anxiety around social situations are known as "social anxiety". Interacting with others can be a source of anxiety for many children and you may notice your child start to avoid spending time with their peers.

While it can be tempting to shield your child from social situations, try to find ways for them to engage with others they feel comfortable with. This might mean seeing one friend at a time and choosing activities with less emphasis on conversation (like the cinema or swimming). You could also help your child develop their friendship skills – like looking for shared interests, asking questions and suggesting activities.

Take it slow – one small, brave step at a time – and remember to offer lots of praise and encouragement. Socializing increases feelings of well-being so, even if it's a scary prospect for your child, they'll feel better for it.

Gut health

Researchers are finding an ever-closer link between gut health and mental health, so it makes sense to ensure your child is getting enough gut-healthy food and drink. Try to include plenty of the following foods in your child's diet:

- Bananas
- Oats
- Unpeeled fruit and vegetables, such as apples and carrots
- Wholegrains
- Probiotic yoghurt

You could add a child-friendly probiotic powder to a smoothie or encourage them to try fermented foods such as sauerkraut or kombucha. It's also a good idea to let them get grubby in the garden, snuggle with your pets and avoid overuse of antibiotic cleaning products – exposure to a wide range of bacteria will help strengthen their gut health too.

Bedtime routine

Getting to sleep can be incredibly hard for anxious children, so an anti-anxiety bedtime routine is a must.

Your child's routine might feature a warm bath infused with some child-friendly lavender-scented bath oil, reading together, a cuddle with you and perhaps some soothing music. Before bed is also an excellent time for journalling (see page 37) as it helps unburden their mind in readiness for sleep.

If your child struggles to drop off, help them get as cosy as possible and put on their favourite audiobook. You could say, "Don't think too much about sleeping. Your body will benefit from rest so all you need to do is snuggle down and concentrate on the story."

Taking the pressure off falling asleep can be the key to helping them relax.

House rules

Call a family meeting and write a list of house rules as a team. Knowing exactly where the boundaries are brings a sense of security which can help calm anxiety.

Every family is different, so think about what's important to you and what will contribute to a harmonious home life.

Try to come up with a set of rules that everyone can agree on and put it up somewhere prominent. Remember, everyone has to stick to the house rules, even grown-ups!

Mirror affirmations

Repeating short, positive sentences beginning with "I am..." or "I can..." has been found to increase self-worth and optimism, calming the mind and helping combat anxiety.

Try decorating your child's mirror (or the bathroom mirror if your child doesn't have their own) with affirmations on Post-it notes.

Here are a few ideas to get you started:

- I am confident.

- I am always trying my best.

- I can do difficult things.

When stuck on a mirror, your child will see these messages every time they see their own face, helping to boost their self-belief.

Chapter 6

SKILLS

FOR

LIFE

In this chapter we'll explore some of those tricky situations that are challenging and anxiety-provoking at any age, and how to give your child some tools and strategies to handle them with confidence and compassion.

Teach conflict resolution

Many parents instinctively try to protect their children from conflict – confrontation is often a source of anxiety for children and adults alike. But by sheltering our children from disagreements, we prevent them from learning a valuable life skill: conflict resolution.

Follow the steps below to help your child find solutions themselves:

1   Let both parties say their piece. If need be, you can help give your child prompts: "I don't like it when..."

2   Avoid blame and repeat back what the problem is.

3   Let your child come up with a solution. If it doesn't work, return to point one.

4   If your child can become comfortable standing up for themselves as well as see the other person's point of view when conflict arises, their confidence will grow and they'll learn they can handle any problem.

Express big emotions safely

Tantrums can be hard to handle and they're certainly not confined to the toddler years! When your child lashes out and loses control of their body, this can be an expression of overwhelming anxiety.

All emotions are OK, but not all behaviour is. If you think your child is going to hurt themselves, another person or someone's property, it's time to address their behaviour and move them to a safe place.

Rather than trying to stop your child's actions entirely, redirect their emotional energy by encouraging them to walk, stomp or growl. This will discharge the big feelings while keeping everybody safe. Letting your child know you have control of the situation can help calm them – you could say something like, "I'm not going to let you hit."

Alternatively, the NHS recommends a number of calming techniques to encourage your child to try, such as: slow breathing, counting to ten, and clenching and unclenching their fists to release tension in the body.

Tricky subjects

Children ask the most awkward questions sometimes, and it's hard to know how to respond. A lot of anxiety can emerge when children know a snippet of truth, so when the inevitable questions about complicated topics like sex, death or politics arise, be honest!

Give your child a straight, accurate and age-appropriate answer. Be ready for sadness or anger – the facts of life can be difficult for a child to accept – and be sure to validate any emotions your child might feel.

If you don't feel confident answering just yet, you could say, "That's a good question. I'll answer you properly when we get home." It's also a good idea to research books on the subject aimed at your child's age range.

How to help your child hold a boundary

Saying "no" is the easy bit. The hard part of your child standing up for themselves is sticking to their guns if the other person doesn't like or respect their "no". This can be a source of great anxiety as it can feel more comfortable to do things they don't want to do in order to avoid conflict.

It's important to teach children about boundaries from as young an age as possible. That their body and mind belong to them, and that if someone is upset by their "no" it doesn't mean they have done something wrong.

Equally, it's essential to instil respect for others' boundaries in your child. Teach them to respect "no" and also that hearing "no" doesn't mean they're a bad person.

School

School can bring a plethora of things to be anxious about. Complex social dynamics, tests, workload, bullying... the list goes on.

Let your child know that you are their ally when it comes to school. Even though you're not there with them day to day, when something is causing them distress take the opportunity to show them you are on their side.

Talk to their teacher or the parents of any other children involved. Ask for changes and brainstorm solutions with your child. Let your child see that you are taking them seriously and sticking up for them, and they will feel safe coming to you with their worries.

Relationships

Whether it's best friends, study buddies, boyfriends, girlfriends or a lack of friends, relationships can bring complication, confusion and anxiety to all our lives from a very young age.

Relationships are of course a source of joy, fun and mutual support as well, and healthy friendships are essential to good mental well-being.

But when conflict arises, it's important your child knows how to deal with it (see page 118). Make sure your child knows that they have a right to feel good in their relationships, that the other person should never hurt them emotionally or physically. Most importantly: it's better to be alone than with someone who doesn't treat you well.

Separation anxiety

Sadly, separation anxiety isn't just for those first days at school. It can come up at almost any age and be quite embarrassing for older children.

There are lots of strategies for easing separation anxiety, from comfort objects to "hug buttons" (a heart drawn on their hand to press when they need a little comfort), but the key to mastering that tricky goodbye moment is to stay calm, empathetic and intuitive. Learning to cope while away from those closest to us is a lifelong skill. The more secure we become in our own abilities and the love of our parents or carers, the more we can master separation.

Mindfulness for children

Mindfulness is about being in the moment and focusing on what you are doing using all of your senses. It can be practised at any time, anywhere, but a simple way to teach mindfulness to children is by using food.

Next time you sit down to eat together, ask your child to look, touch, smell, listen to and taste their food as if it's the first time they've ever seen it. This can be a funny exercise, so do join in and look really carefully at your own food, too.

Mindfulness has been found to improve mood, emotional regulation skills and self-esteem in children and adults alike, while lowering anxiety and stress.

Self-soothing

While comforting your child and being there for them is incredibly important, especially when they are struggling emotionally, the ultimate goal is to help them learn to self-soothe.

This isn't achieved by getting them to "toughen up" and leaving them to do it alone. Refusing comfort simply teaches them not to reach out for help and can lead to unhealthy coping mechanisms.

Children learn to regulate their own emotions best when we give them the tools to recognize their emotional state, so talk about emotions throughout the day (see page 17). If it seems like your child's anxiety is rising, suggest one of their favourite calming activities (see Chapter 2) before they get overwhelmed. The more you model this, the better they'll become at spotting it themselves.

Learning to rest

When there's a lot to do, anxiety can put resting at the bottom of anyone's list of priorities. If your child is feeling overwhelmed by tasks, teach them how to prioritize, how to pace themselves and most crucially how to rest.

You might like to draw a grid for them, breaking the tasks down by urgency, deadline and how long they'll take. Make sure you put breaks on their timetable too, showing that they are just as important as any piece of homework, revision, sports club or project.

Help them work through the tasks one by one, ticking them off as you go.

Tolerating discomfort

Feeling uncomfortable is part of life. The discomfort of being a beginner, for example. Yet our brains naturally want to stop the discomfort and this might cause us to act in a variety of ways, conscious or unconscious, to help us return to familiarity. For instance, we might talk ourselves out of learning a new skill by criticizing our abilities or the value of the skill itself.

Helping your child to understand that they can sit with discomfort and ignore anxious or self-sabotaging thoughts is a useful skill for them to learn. It can help to imagine thoughts and emotions like clouds floating by: we can simply watch them without judging or acting on them, even if they feel uncomfortable.

Once children are able tolerate the discomfort of anxiety and detach from the negative thoughts it brings, they'll find the courage to face their fears.

The opinions of other people

Feeling misunderstood or judged by others is hard. Anxiety about what other people think of us can cause sleepless nights, social isolation and lost friendships.

It's hard, but you can help your child feel understood by actively listening, validating their feelings and telling them that they make sense (see page 12).

You could gently explain to your child that not everyone will like or understand them – imagine how strange it would be to be everyone's best friend – and that despite this they still make sense and are loved by those closest to them.

Staying safe online

Smartphones and social media present a difficult and fast-evolving source of anxiety for our children. The urge to check their phones, even if doing so brings heightened anxiety or bullying, can become an addiction. Smartphones are designed to capture our attention and keep us hooked, yet we *can* arm our kids with the knowledge, tools and critical thinking skills to cultivate a healthy relationship with their online worlds.

A parental control app is a must for making the internet safe enough for your kids. Be open to conversations with your child about the restrictions you choose and be ready to respectfully say "no" to permissions you're not comfortable with.

Show your child how to block, report and put their own screentime boundaries in place. Sit down together to discuss limiting notifications, how social media affects their mood and let them know they can always talk to you if they are ever subject to an uncomfortable or threatening situation online.

Nurture their inner artist

Regardless of your disposition, creativity can and should play a part in everyone's lives at every age. The therapeutic effects of creativity are undeniable, from healing from trauma to reducing stress and anxiety.

To instil creativity early on, let your child see you being creative. Doodle or dance and give no thought to quality or technical skill. Creativity is not about "good" or "bad" – the important things are playfulness and self-expression.

Encourage your child to be creative on their own terms (see page 61) and display their creations around your home with pride.

Cultivating self-trust

Learning to trust themselves will set your child up for life. Just like trust in others, self-trust is earned, so let your child rely on themselves in certain situations in order to prove to themselves that they are trustworthy.

The key to teaching self-trust is recognizing that your child is the expert on themselves. So, as a parent, it's important to avoid telling your child how they feel or should feel. For example, if your child says they're not cold, don't force them to wear a coat. If they insist they don't need the toilet, take their word for it. Giving them autonomy in this way will show them that they can rely on their own judgement and that even if they make a regrettable choice, they can change their mind and learn from their mistakes.

Chapter 7

LOOKING

TO

YOURSELF

Children take a lot of their emotional cues from their parents, so it's necessary to look at our own actions when thinking about our children's emotional well-being. It can be uncomfortable to consider this but always remember that you're doing your best with the knowledge you have and it's never too late to make positive changes.

Breaking a cycle of worry

Children care deeply about their parents – even if they don't always show it. How we respond to their emotions can inform how (and whether) they express them next time. If a child is concerned that their anxiety makes their parents upset, they can feel anxious about expressing it.

This cycle of worry can be hard to break – everyone in the situation feels anxiety about anxiety! The way to solve this is not to supress your own emotions, but to show that you are the adult and your child is not responsible for taking care of your feelings.

You could say, "When I see you having a hard time I do feel worried, and that's OK – I can take care of my feelings. I always want to know what it's like to be you; it's part of my job as a parent to help take care of your feelings."

Identify your stress points

Is there a particular time of day when your child's anxiety is guaranteed to be heightened? It's likely you dread this time, anticipating your child's distress or difficult behaviour in the lead-up. We often can't avoid these parts of the daily routine, but we can make adjustments that lower our own stress and release a little of the pressure.

- If it's leaving the house that's challenging, try getting everyone's shoes on 5 minutes earlier.

- Mealtimes can be a battlefield – could your child serve themselves, so they have a bit of control over what's on their plate?

- If bedtime is a stress point, try taking a bath straight after lights-out. Being unavailable but still close by might help your child relax.

See how you can make your own life a little easier and calmer, and watch that ripple out to your child.

Rethinking "neediness"

Everyone has needs – even parents! Many of us grow up to feel discomfort asking for what we need – be that rest, attention, clarity, a pay rise, an apology – and this leads to an irritation when our children's needs feel like too much.

What can be seen as "neediness" in a child is simply them asking for something. Whether they're seeking your attention or asking for the moon on a stick, try to respond with a generous spirit, even if you're not able or willing to grant their request.

When it's attention your child wants, give it as much as you can – it is essential to them! The more freely you give your child attention, the less they'll feel the need to clamour for it.

Lead by example

Let your child see that you get anxious too. This will help your child see that they are not alone in their feelings.

Try articulating your emotions more – whatever you're feeling! For example, if you're feeling worried about a big meeting at work, talk through your feelings with your child (taking care not to burden them with your worries!) and explain any strategies you're planning to use to lower your anxiety. Most importantly, show your child that you are going to go for it even if it feels scary or risky.

Seeing you being brave will help your child grow their confidence and understand that adults aren't perfect and bravery is a lifelong skill.

Using mindfulness

Coming back to the present moment is an incredibly useful skill. If you can master it, you gain the ability to find calm in any situation. It helps us pause before reacting and keep our cool when dealing with a challenging behaviour.

Try being fully present right now. Feel the air move through your body as you breathe, take notice of the sounds and smells around you and how your clothes feel against your skin.

Next time you feel your stress levels rising due to pressures at work or a tricky parenting situation, come back to this feeling.

Regularly practising mindfulness helps reduce stress and anxiety, as well as improving mood and helping you sleep.

Self-care for parents

Self-care isn't selfish! It's easy to forget yourself when you have small people relying on you, especially when one of those small people is struggling.

You're a human being too and just as worthy of rest, boundaries and fulfilment as anyone else.

Self-care looks different for everyone. Some crave a lie-in while others relish the freedom of a solo run. Letting go of a burdensome responsibility or taking on a new creative hobby might be what you need.

Making time to recharge your batteries so you can be your best, calmest and happiest self will set a good example to your children, and they'll benefit from a healthier, less stressed and more energetic parent.

Rethinking "naughtiness"

What we label "naughty" is often an expression of anxiety and distress. Children lack the capacity to articulate complex emotions and acting out is often the most efficient way to get the attention of the adults around them.

When seen in this light, it can be easier to empathize with your child. Start by reassuring them that they're safe. Try to name the emotion: "I think you're feeling worried, am I right?" Just be near them, as calmly and quietly as you can.

When difficult emotions are met with empathy rather than resistance, your child will feel understood, loved and accepted.

Saying sorry

All parents mess up sometimes. We raise our voices, make threats we don't intend to carry out or use hurtful language. First of all, forgive yourself. You are only human.

When we make parenting mistakes, the most important thing is to repair your relationship with your child.

Apologize, make amends, explain your actions and emphasize that your child did not deserve or cause what happened.

In doing this, you re-establish trust between yourself and your child. You are also teaching them how to articulate emotions and how to behave when they make a mistake or hurt someone.

Practise acceptance

A lot of frustration can come from trying to resist how your child is feeling or what they are telling you. It's easy to feel like you're failing as a parent if your child is struggling. But, to accept the present does not mean you are happy with it or that you don't want to change it. Try to let go of the impulse to minimize, deny or catastrophize what your child is going through. They are a complex, imperfect human being just like you.

When you accept the present situation, you free up your mind to work on solutions rather than stressing about how you got here.

Be kind to yourself

Notice how you speak about yourself and the world around you – what do you tell yourself when you make a mistake? How about when you think about something new you'd like to try?

If you have a harsh or critical inner voice it can be very uncomfortable to start challenging it. Speaking positively can feel inauthentic or counter-intuitive.

The way we view ourselves and how we understand the world is very influential on our children. Your child subconsciously picks up on your worldview and absorbs these messages, creating their own inner voice.

Start with what you say out loud: find something positive to say about yourself when you look in the mirror, instead of looking for faults. Speak hopefully about a new venture, instead of predicting failure.

Chapter 8

GETTING

HELP

You might decide that outside help is the best choice for your child. This is personal to every family, so trust your own judgement. Reaching out for support of any kind is a sign of strength and love for your child – you should never feel guilt or shame for doing so.

When to ask for help

There's no wrong or right time to ask for outside help. If your child's mental health is having a negative effect on their life, reaching out for extra support is a good idea.

A lot of parents are concerned about being seen as oversensitive by medical professionals. There's also a myth that ignoring anxiety will mean it goes away by itself. If you're thinking along these lines, try to let that go!

Start by talking to your child's school and your family doctor. They'll be able to advise the next steps. Alternatively, you could go directly to a therapist to discuss your concerns.

Self-help

Self-help books can be a great resource to better equip ourselves for parenting, whether or not you decide to seek outside help. There are lots out there for both adults and children; here are some I'd personally recommend:

For adults:

Can We Talk? by Dr Sarah Vohra

The Book You Wish Your Parents Had Read by Philippa Perry

It's OK Not to Share by Heather Shumaker

Good Inside by Dr Becky Kennedy

The Whole-Brain Child by Dr Daniel Siegel and Dr Tina Payne Bryson

For children:

A Handful of Quiet by Thích Nhất Hạnh

Healthy, Happy Minds by The School of Life

Starving the Anxiety Gremlin by Kate Collins-Donnelly

Don't Worry, Be Happy by Poppy O'Neill

Talking to your child about professional help

If you decide to make an appointment to see your doctor, make sure you let your child know what is going to happen at every stage. Involve them in decision-making, listen to any concerns they may have, validate and reassure them. Treat it just as you would if you were seeking help for a physical health problem.

The doctor will likely ask questions about school, home life, relationships and physical health as well as their thoughts and feelings.

Let them know that it's OK to be uncertain, it's OK to take a break and it's OK to say "no" to anything they don't feel comfortable with.

Preparing for a visit to your doctor

It's helpful to keep a record of how anxiety affects your child across the space of a week or a number of days. You might like to score emotions out of ten or keep a diary or mood tracker – together with your child or separately – for this purpose.

If visiting the doctor is a source of anxiety for your child, try role-playing the appointment with them, then switching roles. As always: listen, validate and reassure your child.

Arranging a treat for straight after the appointment – like a movie night or hot chocolate together in a café – can sometimes help, too.

Making decisions

It can be hard to know the right thing to do for your child when they're struggling, especially if you're involving the opinions of professionals. The acronym BRAIN can help:

Benefits – what are the benefits of this decision?

Risks – what are the risks involved?

Alternatives – what are the alternatives?

Intuition – what is your gut feeling?

Nothing – what if we do nothing, or wait and see?

Know that you are the one who knows your child best, and it's important to involve and discuss any decisions relating to their care with your child.

Taking a holistic approach

While your child's emotional well-being is the top priority during times of crisis, it's also worth looking at your child's lifestyle holistically. Ensuring every part of your child's life is as healthy as possible will help them grow into strong, emotionally intelligent young people.

Make sure your child has plenty of:

- Play

- Sleep

- Time in nature

- Exercise

- Quiet time

- Friends

- Family time

- Access to books

- Access to creative materials

If you think your child is lacking in any of these areas, look at how you might add more of it to their daily life. There are lots of ideas in this book for inspiration!

Types of help available

There are a number of different forms of support and therapy your child might benefit from, including play therapy, art therapy, psychotherapy, animal therapy, cognitive behavioural therapy (CBT), mindfulness and family therapy.

What's available to you will depend on where you live, your child's individual needs and your personal circumstances. Speak to your doctor and your child's school, have a look around locally and turn to parents who've been in a similar situation for recommendations.

Reach out

When your child is struggling with anxiety, it can take a lot out of you. Make sure you as parents have plenty of support, too. It can be hard to ask for help initially, but just know that those who care about you will want to be there for you.

You could get the grandparents to babysit, book in a coffee with your closest friends or perhaps find a therapist to help support you through what can be a difficult time.

Letting off steam and talking about how you're feeling and how the experience is affecting you will lighten your load and help you feel less alone.

Looking to the future

Anxiety is a normal part of a healthy emotional life, so eradicating it completely from your child's mind is neither possible nor desirable. The aim is to give your child the tools to deal with normal anxiety when it arises, and to know how to recognize and ask for help if it becomes overwhelming.

You might like to offer extra support in times of change or stress such as starting a new school, moving house, puberty or exams, as these can trigger a rise in anxiety levels.

Remember to always trust your gut and talk to your child about emotions regularly – the good and the bad.

Conclusion

I hope you have found some inspiration and encouragement in this book. There's no one-size-fits-all solution to anxiety, because every human mind is different. By acknowledging your child's struggles and looking for guidance, you're giving them the best chance at mastering anxiety and growing into a mentally strong, resilient and emotionally healthy adult.

As awareness of mental health is growing, so is acceptance. Always remember that your child is not alone and neither are you. Every time you speak with honesty and empathy is an act of bravery and love.

Keep going!

Resources and Further Reading

The Book You Wish Your Parents Had Read
by Philippa Perry

Can We Talk? by Dr Sarah Vohra

It's OK Not to Share by Heather Shumaker

Wreck This Journal by Keri Smith

Starving the Anxiety Gremlin by Kate Collins-Donnelly

Don't Worry, Be Happy by Poppy O'Neill

www.youngminds.org.uk/parent/parents-helpline-and-webchat

www.childmind.org/topics/anxiety

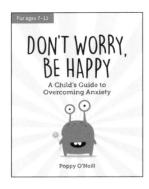

DON'T WORRY, BE HAPPY

A Child's Guide to
Overcoming Anxiety

Poppy O'Neill

Paperback

ISBN: 978-1-78685-236-6

This practical guide for children aged 7–11 combines proven cognitive-behavioural therapy methods and fun and engaging activities, which are interspersed with useful tips, inspirational statements and practical information for parents, to help your child overcome anxiety.

MY WORRY JOURNAL

Write Away Your Worries and Chill
Out with Some Calming Activities

Paperback

ISBN: 978-1-80007-720-1

Everyone worries – it's a normal part of life – but whenever it feels a bit too much we need to stop, take a breath, and do something fun! *My Worry Journal* is for those times. It contains a fabulous selection of activities, with doodling pages designed to help children cope with feelings of worry.

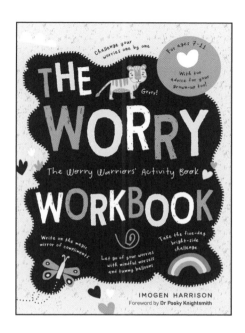

THE WORRY WORKBOOK

The Worry Warriors' Activity Book

Imogen Harrison

Paperback   ISBN: 978-1-78783-537-5

Worries come in all shapes and sizes and can creep up on us when we least expect them, stopping us from doing the things we really want and spoiling our fun. *The Worry Workbook* is here to help by explaining what worry is, offering creative ways to calm and distract yourself when worry strikes.

Have you enjoyed this book?

If so, why not write a review on your favourite website?

If you're interested in finding out more about our books,
find us on Facebook at **Summersdale Publishers**,
on Twitter at **@Summersdale** and on Instagram and
TikTok at **@summersdalebooks** and get in touch.
We'd love to hear from you!

Thanks very much for buying this Summersdale book.

www.summersdale.com